Evelyn Threlfall

Starlight Songs

Evelyn Threlfall

Starlight Songs

ISBN/EAN: 9783337408565

Printed in Europe, USA, Canada, Australia, Japan

Cover: Foto ©Thomas Meinert / pixelio.de

More available books at **www.hansebooks.com**

STARLIGHT SONGS

BY

EVELYN THRELFALL

*" Thou clearest Star of all the throng,
Above dim sea and shadowy shore,
Take thou this broken gift of song;
Alas! that I can give no more."*

LONDON
KEGAN PAUL, TRENCH, TRÜBNER, & CO. Lᵗᴰ
PATERNOSTER HOUSE, CHARING CROSS ROAD
1895

OVERTURE

Stars! as gold in the mines of night,
Stars, as joys on the face of pain,
Look on us, who remember again
Morning and noontide vanished from sight.
Where is the Sun-god's glory and might,
The three-fold arch at the gates of rain,
The rippled cloudlets light and white,
The green of grass, and the gold of grain?
Where is the day at whose heart we have lain?
But the ear of Night makes all prayers vain !

What of the morrows that, glad or weeping,
Tread the old paths to the one old end ?—
Rushes, over our graves that bend,
Bow to earth at their wings' wide sweeping,
Sand upon dust is Time upheaping
As drops of rain with a river blend ;
And the winged days touch not our place of sleeping,
With lips grown languid to foe and friend,

OVERTURE

We blame no more what the gods may send,
The once rent robe they may not rend;
What shall our loss be, what our gain?
But the ear of Night makes all prayers vain!

Children glad to the pale night born,
Fair star-children, only you
Out of the deep dusk dank with dew
Shine on us, speak to us, us forlorn
With feet way-weary and garments torn,
No prize but sleep for our soul's due;
Though noontide gave us burning scorn
And purple grief was the twilight's hue,
You, silver-speared, one hope pursue,
Join hands, and stretch from the old to the new,
The new day, born without sorrow or stain!
But the ear of Night makes all prayers vain!

Are you souls of joys dead long ago,
Joys that weep on the breast of God,
Weep for glad gardens yet untrod
At the first fierce breath of the wind and snow;
Though life-germs slumber their feet below,
Even where the death frost nips the sod,
They may not welcome them, for they go
Where by dark streams pale poppies nod.

OVERTURE

For the lips of Love have kissed the rod
And his feet go down into Hell unshod,
Shall no crown in the end for his cross remain?
But the ear of Night makes all prayers vain!

We dreamed Life different, aye, and Death
A dream, a trance, but not a grave;
New worlds we looked for, strong and brave
For Heaven above, or Hell beneath.
But as the rose dies in yon wreath
We die, and Earth receives, who gave.
Rust, warrior's sword, within the sheath!
Lie still, dry brush, dead craftsman's slave!
The hands that wielded, no more crave
Through you the crowns that could not save,
They sow, they go—Fate reaps the grain,
But the ear of Night makes all prayers vain!

Stars, you are above, and beneath, the sea,
Sea that spreads to the far South Pole,
Thither the following billows roll,
Thither the gull flies, and is free,
But oh, sweet stars, 'twixt you and me,
A greater grief outstrips control
And is not measured as this may be.
No waves waft onward the pilgrim soul,

Her guiding chart is an empty scroll,
She shall sink, sink, sink, from her stars, her goal,
To the depths of space, where the worlds refrain,
Oh Night! good-night, if our prayers be vain!

Stars of the South we call you ; yet,
South and North and East and West
Are one to your cold eternal rest,
To your eyes that watch years rise and set
With bitter longing and mad regret,
The lives of men unguided, unblest,
The dust of Earth that the years forget.
See yonder, over the black hill crest,
The light of a cross on Night's mournful breast,
The cross with the crown in Heaven, seen best
By wanderers burnt with the red sun-stain.
Oh Night! good-night, if our prayers be vain!

Lo, yon half shut magnolia flower
That in dark foliage dimly hides,
Robed in white beauty like a bride's,
Is queen of all the moonlit hour ;
Not England's rose, her June's best dower,
In whose warm heart the bee abides,
Wins memory back, as from dark bower
The great white star uncurls, divides,

OVERTURE

As if some wave of heavenly tides
Had washed a planet to Earth's sides,
Oh living star, oh perfumed pain!
Oh Night! good-night, if our prayers be vain!

Oh stars of mine, draw me homeward still,
Home to the breast of night and peace,
Till the sounds of Life grow faint and cease,
And the world that spins like a wheeling mill
Drops out of sight's way over the hill,
And pillowed safe in a soft cloud's crease
The tired soul lies and sleeps his fill.
Though God should give for the world's release
The mystic Lamb of the silver fleece,
His blood renews no lifetime's lease,
Nor brings one dead joy back again.
Oh Night! good-night, if our prayers be vain!

Dear stars, Eternity has kissed
Your pale cold eyes that gaze and gaze,
And pass not from the deathless ways,
Where sapphire burns to amethyst
Beyond the heaven of heavens—yet list,
Eternal, to one winged moth's praise,
Who not one hour may Fate resist,
My heart close up to your own heart raise

Beyond the burden of nights and days,
Life's footsteps pass, but the throned Love stays
The changeless Love at whose heart we have lain.
Oh Night, good-night, for our prayers are vain !

CONTENTS

		PAGE
I.	AT EDEN'S GATE	13
II.	ODE TO SYDNEY HARBOUR	18
III.	WHEN WE PARTED	24
IV.	THE ROAD TO FERN TREE SPRING	30
V.	WALTZ MUSIC	36
VI.	TO C. R. F. T.	41
VII.	THE PASSION FLOWER	46
VIII.	THE OFFERING	51
IX.	THE ROSE	53
X.	THE ROSE AND THE STAR	54
XI.	THE TEMPLE OF FAME	56
XII.	A SONG OF A GARDEN	59
XIII.	A SONG OF LOVE AND DEATH	61
XIV.	REMEMBRANCE	62
XV.	A MELODY	64
XVI.	A REQUIEM	65
XVII.	"SI JEUNESSE SAVAIT"	66
XVIII.	TO A BABY	67
XIX.	AT A LIFE'S END	69
XX.	THROUGH HOPE TO SLEEP	72
XXI.	AN ANTHEM OF MORTALITY	74

CONTENTS

		PAGE
XXII.	SONNET—PYGMALION'S DREAM	76
XXIII.	SONNET—THE FULFILMENT	77
XXIV.	SONNET	78
XXV.	SONNET	79
XXVI.	LIFE	80
XXVII.	FAILURE	81
XXVIII.	IN THE GARDEN OF THE SHADOW	83
XXIX.	RONDEL	85
XXX.	RONDEL	86
XXXI.	RONDEL	87
XXXII.	RONDEL	88
XXXIII.	SERENADE	89
XXXIV.	HVMN	92
XXXV.	SUNSET-LAND	95
XXXVI.	SONNET—GOOD-NIGHT	97
XXXVII.	ENVOI	98

STARLIGHT SONGS

I

AT EDEN'S GATE

"With footsteps faltering on the strand,
We lean on Thee, and weep to part;
The gift of Life is in Thy hand,
The sword of Death is in our heart."

LOVE is henceforth the light
That turns to day the night,
   Starless and cold;
In that eternal dawn,
On dewy wood and lawn,
   His flowers unfold.

A world not Heaven, nor Earth,
Sweet at the springtide's birth
   With young green leaves;
Till suns, of summer lit,
Make gold the face of it
   With harvest sheaves

The rose is red in June,
The lark has no such tune
    As here he sings;
Springtime and Summer here
Glide round, nor dies the year
    On wintry wings.

They who have entered in
Are souls from strife and sin
    New-born to God,
Our God, whose word is love,
Rung through the sacred grove
    His feet have trod.

Their white robes brush the grass
That bendeth as they pass
    With flowers weighed down;
By waters calm as peace
They find, where wanderings cease,
    Their starry crown.

The mystic morning breaks
And heart on heart awakes
    With waking flowers;
A world they have not known
Is ever more their own
    In all its hours.

AT EDEN'S GATE

Oh years too short to hold
All dreams of days of old,
    All hopes to come !
Oh meadows where we dwell,
Of rose and asphodel,
    Oh happy home !

Our only God and Lord
Not he, of saints adored
    In Nazareth ;
But Thou, oh more Divine,
We take Thy bread and wine
    For life or death.

Lo Time, and Fate, and Chance
Ever their awful dance
    Lead on, still on ;
Ah, what are we to them—
We, who that tide would stem,
    And then—are gone !

But Thou, not born of Earth,
Who art 'twixt Death and Birth,
    'Twixt joy and pain ;
Thou only friend of man,
Undimmed Thy face we scan
    While tear-drops rain.

Oh draw us nearer yet
Where souls, like stars, are set
    Around Thy shrine;
Where, vaulted by deep skies,
Thine altar flames arise,
    Their glories shine.

No voice like Thine, no sway,
Whose service night and day
    Is only song:
The music of all spheres
Transcribed to mortal ears
    A sweet life long.

*   *   *   *   *

And yet we weep; so brief
'Twixt green and falling leaf
    So brief the time;
Though joys of ages meet
In one sublime heart's beat,
    One kiss sublime.

Our love, so lately born,
That looks in ways unworn
    His steps to trace;
Our love, not ours, but paid
Where springtime fields are made
    A desert place.

His myrtle flowers even now
Twine with the cypress bough
   To wreath his head,
And from immortal lips
Deep tears those words eclipse
   The sweetest said.

Ah, by the thunders of the strand
   From thee, from thee, how shall we part!
The gift of Life is in Thy hand,
   The sword of Death is in our heart!

II

ODE TO SYDNEY HARBOUR

Here I look thee over,
  Sister of the sea,
And thy languid sleep discover
In the arms of Earth thy lover,
  With the skies for canopy.

Now my spirit trembles
  Face to face with thee,
For what beauty thine resembles,
In whose mask dark Fate dissembles,
  What hath been and what shall be?

In Earth's green embraces,
  Sister of the sea,
Sleep, and dream of future races,
Treading down thy far high places,
  Where no footstep yet might be.

ODE TO SYDNEY HARBOUR

There's a time for slumber,
   Thine awhile may be,
Till the years their full tide number,
Till Time's path thou dost encumber,
   And his wide wings shadow thee.

Sapphire at sun-shining,
   Opal at sunset,
In day-dawn or day-declining
Green grey robes with rose-red lining,
   And a red-gold coronet.

And at night resplendent
   Rise the great white moons,
Through the steel-blue deeps ascendant,
High above thy darkness pendant,
   Brighter than the blaze of noons.

There's a pure bright highway
   Leading into space,
Who shall tread it? nay, but I may,
Sea-ward, star-ward, is it my way
   To the soul's abiding-place?

Night, ablaze with glory,
   And alive with wings!
Hearts grown weary, heads grown hoary,
Live in thy romantic story
   Feasted from thy living springs.

ODE TO SYDNEY HARBOUR

Thou hast many morrows,
   I have but to-day,
But thy star-robed sadness borrows,
From their endless joys and sorrows,
   Who are born and pass away.

Thou wilt whisper lowly
   Unto them as me,
Words that make life glad and holy,
Till they fain would cry, "Creep slowly,
   Stream of Time, towards the sea!"

Swift their time of blooming,
   Swift their joyless end,
Food for thankless Death's consuming,
Shells of yonder seas' entombing,
   Shells the great waves seize and rend.

On thy vast blue ceiling
   Stars their history write,
But for ever unrevealing,
Wide-eyed sphinx to all appealing,
   Thou dost watch the face of Night.

Still thy breast untired
   Nurses Heaven asleep,
Heaven—where never soul aspired
Seeking out the crown desired—
   Falls upon thine heart to weep.

Whirling realms of nations
    Are as nought to thee,
Latest of all Earth's creations!
Southern stars from their high stations
    Saw thee born of air and sea.

Mirror of eternal
    Days that are as years:—
In thy grasp are powers infernal,
But a forest garland vernal
    Is the robe thy queendom wears.

From thy wisdom's treasure
    Canst thou tell us this,
Shall a few years' pain or pleasure
Be of Love and Life the measure,
    See the end of all that is?

With calm eyes beholding
    All the things that be,
Tell us some sweet truth worth holding
Of the wings of God enfolding,
    Souls that Death shall but set free.

But thy silence teaches
    In a tongue unknown,
Man that wonders and beseeches,
Man that unto Godhead reaches,
    Hath the grave for Godhead's throne.

Peace! the dusk is dreary,
   Yet the noon is bright,
Flash thy purple wings, glad Peri,
Till the eyes of Love wax weary,
   Till the soul finds rest in night.

III

WHEN WE PARTED

STILL the cattle in the pasture wander through the long, warm days,
And the mournful gum trees rustle in the forest's ferny maze,
And the woodland scents and music, that will haunt me till I die,
Bring me back the hour long years since, when we parted, you and I.

Maiden of the wind-swept pasture, grown to wife and motherhood,
Leaving in the years behind you, passion dimly understood!
When you wedded I could bear it, for the worst was done before,
When I loved you, yes, and left you, and in leaving loved you more;
But I lacked the faith to keep you, faith in your heart and my own,
Left you doubting, left you, lost you—oh my love, had I but known!
For I know now that you loved me, dreamed me false and gave your life,

Loveless, to another's keeping, who could dare to call
   you "wife!"
And you live in peace and honour, never shall our paths
   unite,
And you bear unto another children that were mine
   by right,—
Mine, if I had known my riches, kept the heart I knew
   too late,
Then I had not wandered lonely by the cold dark seas
   of Fate,—
Lonely, loveless,—for the memory of your slightest smile
   or sigh
Blots out all the world of women since we parted, you
   and I.

"Never trust the love of women!" cried a voice
   within my heart,
And I listened, and I watched you, dreaming that you
   played a part,
And our first long kiss at evening grew a phantom by
   the morn,
And the words the pure stars taught us were the brazen
   sunlight's scorn;
Though your arms around me bound me to your mouth
   of flowerlike red,
And your fragrant hair blown round me as a rose's scent
   was shed,

And your white breast warmly beating, passion shaken for my sake!
Till your kisses conquered reason—I could dream and never wake!
All the night looked pale with passion—all the morrow cold with doubt,
And your voice was drowned in noises echoing from the world without;
Till one morn came cold and jealous, froze my heart and bade me fly,
Cursèd, cruel voice that called me when we parted, you and I!

Where the waving rushes whisper, down beside the stagnant creek,
We would watch the red sun setting on the distant mountain peak,
And your face had caught a radiance from the rose-clouds in the west,
And your burning eyes were shadowed as you veiled them on my breast;
Oh better had I borne you over purple hills afar,
To the seas that slumber never, out beyond the evening star,
From the green Australian pastures to the wondrous worlds of old,
To the paths of Fate's directing and the years that should unfold,—

WHEN WE PARTED

Hair wherein the sun was woven! pale lips burned to
    passion's red!
Was my happy heart your pillow once, oh jasmine-
    scented head?
Once, and never more for ever! Fate's unfathomed
    waters lie
'Twixt my heart and you who loved me, when we parted,
    you and I.

Would that your white arms had bound me, chained me
    always to your side,
That I might not turn and wander over deserts waste
    and wide;
Had you known the word to stay me, known to speak
    your inmost heart,
These lone hills and this dull river never could have
    seen us part!
How should you have known my longing when myself
    I did not know,
How should you have bid me linger when I bade myself
    to go!
Darling, you were but a woman, slow to read man's
    changeful mind,
Knowing not your beauty's power, nor its strength to
    hold and bind,
And you took my sentence meekly, as the slave of my desire,
Knowing not one word might quicken all my smoulder-
    ing heart to fire;

Had you chosen, you had broken all my chains and
    set me free,
You had been my life for ever—heart and soul and mind
    of me!
We had faced our fate together, welcoming its good
    or ill,
Onward through the deep green valley, onward to the
    frozen hill,
Pilgrims from the dawn to sunset, led by Eros golden-
    winged,
Passing through the gates of evening, where the sun
    hangs purple-ringed,
Passing to the Night eternal, night unvexed of dream
    or sound,
As a perfect flower will perish, stamped and silent in the
    ground;
—But Life's tree will never blossom nor his chalice brim
    with wine!
Let the night endure for ever, once the day were mine
    and thine!
—But it is not, no nor shall be, we shall die, who never
    lived,
Stronger is the love that holds us than the dim faith
    half believed;
Love is Life, and we have missed it, turned away when
    he drew nigh,
Joy was offered for our taking—but we parted, you
    and I!

Now the sky grows grey above me, and the wheeling curlew cries,
"Love is not the good we dreamed of—Life is fashioned out of lies!"
I have lost you, who so loved you, who shall love you till I die,
And forget at last that ever we were parted, you and I.

IV

THE ROAD TO FERN TREE SPRING

Upon the road to Fern Tree Spring
   The cool ferns rustled in the wood,
When I rode forth to gain a thing
   That was to me Life's only good.
Oh Love so lightly understood!
   Oh last gleam of a golden wing!
I may not ride now, though I would,
   Upon the road to Fern Tree Spring.

The deep, cool stillness after rain,
   The fragrant earth, the dripping trees,
The road still winding to attain
   The far-off mountain's mysteries,
The dappled shade the boughs would fling—
   My dream of joy endeared all these,
Upon the road to Fern Tree Spring.

Till, all the long miles nigh rode through,
   I saw her standing by the fence

To greet me with a shyness new,
   A heavenly coldness of pretence.
She knew the gift I came to bring,
   She knew I loved her, soul and sense,
Upon the road to Fern Tree Spring.

She stood between the day and night,
   Between red sunset and pale moon,
Her head drooped in the mystic light
   As droops a lily in the noon;
Her voice was low and faltering,
   Her beauty made my senses swoon,
Upon the road to Fern Tree Spring.

I leaped from off my horse in haste
   (The moon grew bright, the day waxed pale)
The world without was but a waste,
   I feared to let her power prevail,
Yet spoke, on reason's backward swing,
   I kissed her, by the paddock rail,
Upon the road to Fern Tree Spring.

Oh unforgotten moment! won
   From out the clutch of ruthless Fate!
I clasped her close, my only one,
   The mistress of my love and hate,

My heart that gold head pillowing,—
   Ah me, ah me, we lingered late
Upon the road to Fern Tree Spring.

I rode away before the morn,
   I rode to win her wealth and fame;
Her love should never turn to scorn,
   Her pride should be to bear my name.
For I would conquer Life, and bring
   All gifts to feed that altar flame
Upon the road to Fern Tree Spring.

I whispered close to her pale mouth
   One year should see me claim my bride,
Then East and West and North and South
   I fought the cold, fierce ocean-tide;
One gold tress twisted in a ring
   Was all my token of that ride
Upon the road to Fern Tree Spring.

For her I fought, for her I won,
   I came, when Summer's golden haze
Lay on this land that loves the sun,
   The land of pastoral, peaceful days.
Straight as a shaft flies from the string
   I passed along the old, old ways
Upon the road to Fern Tree Spring.

THE ROAD TO FERN TREE SPRING

I drew so near our meeting-place,
    I dreamed I kissed her lips again;
Then, ah! I saw her living face,
    Her grey eyes washed with purple stain,
Her shape, her light, swift footsteps' swing,
    Her loosened tresses' golden grace,
Upon the road to Fern Tree Spring.

But, oh! just gods! even more than this
    I saw, and better were she dead!
A stranger came that face to kiss,
    And laughed, and stroked that sunlit head:
Even now I feel the serpent sting
    That turned the azure sky blood-red,
Upon the road to Fern Tree Spring.

I held my hand—I did not slay;
    Oh, woman, you were pale with fear!
"I was the fool," you cried that day;
    "I left you for a whole long year,
As if you were a flower to fling
    Aside for months!"—I had faint cheer
Upon the road to Fern Tree Spring.

For so you spoke when he was gone,
    And I rode up and faced you there;
Ah, well, poor reed that I leaned on,
    You have some sorrow for your share!

I think your guardian saint took wing
    When you grew false through sheer despair,
Upon the road to Fern Tree Spring.

Ah, better you had died, in truth;
    And I—I dreamed of death that hour;
But in a flash, my stricken youth,
    My slain love, faded like a flower.
I saw what gifts the years might bring:
    Great truths should crush that falsehood's power
Upon the road to Fern Tree Spring.

So forward! to outlive the lie,
    Far from your false white arms and breast,
Though I shall carry till I die
    The fierce regret that cannot rest.
Though love has grown a worthless thing,
    I see you always, golden tressed,
Upon the road to Fern Tree Spring.

I see you always, though again
    I shall not clasp your perjured hand;
Though love survive, betwixt us twain
    For ever more the fierce gods stand!
Farewell! for myriad voices sing
    From shore to shore, though none remain
Upon the road to Fern Tree Spring.

THE ROAD TO FERN TREE SPRING

Farewell, farewell! Had you been true,
   Even life had been not much to miss,
But now—a few more years lived through,
   And we forget the pang of this.
—Death's starry silence shall not bring
   One promise precious as your kiss
Upon the road to Fern Tree Spring!

V

WALTZ MUSIC

ROUND and round,
    As the world swings, so swing we
    Planets in one course set free;
Come what may, this hour has found
    My heart beating close to thee.

Circle on,
    Faint not, fair feet silken shod,
    That upon my heart have trod!
Till day break and night be gone,
    Circle still my sun, my god!

Long, how long
    I have waited till this hour
    Bring my life to perfect flower;
I have suffered scorn and wrong;
    Fled, but could not flee thy power.

WALTZ MUSIC

If I go,
   Empty is the world beyond;
   Dead as if a wizard's wand
Wrought a moon-cold waste of snow,
   Where her face shines not, fierce or fond.

If in dreams
   I behold her, she who keeps
   Love a slave that laughs or weeps,
Life a glass of swift sand-streams,
   Time a chasm Hope o'erleaps—

If my face,
   Pressed to hers, makes sleep divine
   As a draught of charmèd wine
(Though not mine that happy place,
   And that pillow sweet not mine)—

Yet the ghost
   Of the rapture that I have not
   Far outrules the lips I crave not
Of the rose-crowned maiden host,
   Lips whose kisses lose not, save not!

If I wake
   To her cold and careless glance,
   There's a warm white breast the dance
Stirs to panting breaths that shake
   All the outer walls of chance.

White is she,
    White as snow, as fire is white,
    As a star-flame in the night,
Only burning cold to me,
    Scorching to a nearer sight.

If I span
    With my arm that slender shape,
    In the dance there's no escape;
Let her fly me if she can,
    Though the gulf of Judgment gape!

Near, so near,
    Wheeling thus, I breathe her breath,
    And the earth whirls underneath
With a joy as deep as fear,
    Awful as the kiss of death.

Oh, my own!
    (Since one moment with my arm
    I may hold thee as a charm,
Call thy beauty mine alone,
    Circle, circling thee from harm.)

Time that flies,
    Shall not give this hour again;
    Love that wanes as moons that wane,
Faints not ever in thine eyes,
    If thy breast his head disdain.

From thy scorn,
   He may seek some refuge still,
   Over valley, over hill,
Through the night and on to morn,
   And thy day break lone and chill.

Then in vain,
   Vain to call him name on name,
   With wide eyes and lips aflame,
Shall to-night return again,
   To-morrow night, and be the same?

No, be wise,
   Dear brown eyes that gaze as though
   Slumbered still the spirits' glow,
Ere its sun of Love arise:
   Who shall ever love thee so?

Better now,
   Now to take a whole life's gift,
   Than to wait with watchful thrift,
And a white-wreathed maiden brow,
   As the slow days deathward drift.

On thy breast
   Pale tuberoses faint are drooping;
   I will give thee for thy stooping
Orange flowers of golden crest,
   In white robes as angels grouping.

Bronze-brown hair!
    They shall wreathe thee, crown thee, make
    Monarch of thee for my sake!
Thou a woman art and fair,
    To a woman's queendom wake!

Round and round,
    White and warm and silken-swathed,
    As a fragrant flower is spathed,
Perfumed tresses lily-crowned,
    All in golden radiance bathed.

Round and round!
    Till the world whirls out of sight,
    And the stars dance in the night,
—Round my heart a serpent wound,
    Long and supple, warm and white.

Round and round!
    So the music leads us ever;
    As two leaves float down a river,
We are vanquished by the sound:
    Closer cling—oh! leave me never.

Round and round!
    So I clasp thine hand, and draw
    Thy soul homewards by Love's law,
Till two spirits lost and found,
    Grow one being without flaw.

VI

TO C. R. F. T.

THOU that hast my name,
   Son of my own heart!
Six months now since came
Voice of thee to claim
Life of flickering flame
   In the lamp thou art.

Lamp of God new-lit,
   Burning clear and small,
Like a tiny bit
Of heaven—the joy of it
Heaven's own joy would fit:
   God through Love is all!

Little heart that lay
   Beating close to mine,
When the storms of day,
Rolling far away,
Left thee there to stay
   In the still starshine.

When the mists of pain
　　Floated from the world,
Clear were heart and brain,
Seeing all my gain,
Rosebud pure from stain,
　　In my arm upcurled.

Flower of gardens fair
　　Eye has never seen;
Thou to be my care,
Nestling softly there,
Angels could not share,
　　Nor God come between.

Only women know,
　　Out of bitter stress,
Out of helpless woe,
All the warmth, the glow,
All the blood's glad flow,
　　All the tenderness.

Tiny nut-brown head!
　　Tiny dreaming eyes!
Face on kisses fed,
Wavering arms outspread,
Love, with no speech said,
　　Unto Love replies.

TO C. R. F. T.

With thy growth Love grows
   As the months go on;
And thy spirit knows
Refuge from its woes,
Finding safe repose,
   On my heart alone.

Softest, gentlest thing!
   With a head of down,
Cheek like silken wing
Of a bird of spring,
Even too small to sing,
   Fluffed with feathers brown.

Yet, if life should last,
   Grows the babe to youth;
Youth is overpast,
Manhood comes at last,
Striving to hold fast
   All its pride of truth.

And thy way may lead,
   Even so far, my own—
Then, no help in need:
Fate has once decreed,
Men, in word and deed,
   Stand or fall alone.

Other hearts may beat
　　At the sight of thee,
But thou wilt not meet
Her whose kiss would greet
Tiny, rose-leaf feet
　　Curled upon her knee!

Times and times again
　　Changing Love will veer;
But my joy and pain,
Fixed in thee remain,
And I still would fain
　　Keep my baby here.

Years shall bear thee far
　　From these arms of mine;
Death shall set a bar
Where our pathways are—
Thou with Fame for star,
　　I with Sleep for shrine.

"Mother" call me yet
　　In thy heart that day;
Though my sun be set,
Though mine eyes forget
Love's divine regret,
　　"Mother" only, say.

TO C. R. F. T.

God be with my son!
   Till the morn wax day,
Till the day be done,
And the night begun
Calls the weary one
   From his toil away.

And should my long night
   Call me ere I know,
Let the words I write
Speak as farewells might,
Arming thee for fight,
   Kissing back thy woe.

If thou gain'st a wreath
   Past the dreaming of,
Shall I hear who saith
"This was of thy breath,"
—Lying underneath?
—Love beholds not death,
   Seeing only Love.

VII

THE PASSION FLOWER

My sisters, I am weary! the feet of Time are slow,
In starless paths and dreary, in dawnless ways of woe.
The long, long night of weeping, that counts my tears as pearls,
Forgets the glad god sleeping with flowers on golden curls;
Forgets the day departed, our hope, desire, and crown,
That left us not faint-hearted what time the sun went down.
The night-watch of our sorrow the stars of God should share;
On us should gleam the morrow, more glad than Hope or Prayer!
But Night, oh! sister flowers; Night lives, and Day sleeps sound,
Grey dust of rapturous hours lies thick upon the ground;

Blossoms that spread and scatter, pale leaves kissed white by Death,
Though day should come, what matter! it gives not back their breath!
The dead day lies in ashes, a burnt-out fire of Life;
The distant lightning flashes, but not for Hope or Strife;
For us the cold rain falling, still falling through the dark,
No voice through shadows calling, no star's hope-kindling spark,
But heavy Night that crushes, but deadly Night that kills!
The moan of wind-blown rushes, the rush of rain-swelled rills;
Pale faces upward staring through grasses drenched and dank,
What hand once poured unsparing the purple wine they drank?
The wine that flowed at daybreak, the cup o'erturned at eve,
Broken as clods of clay break—who gave? who shall receive?
Shall any voice have pity, shall any hear at last?—
Within a cold grey city He binds Hope hard and fast.
Alas, my sister-flowers, bow down your heads to earth—
These perfumed lives of ours, born with the morning's birth,

Our purple robes of passion, our crowns of living joy,
The hand so great to fashion is greater to destroy:
The green leaves weep around me, the rain falls on my breast,
The shadow of Death hath found me: I too go with the rest.

My sister-spirits flutter as leaves upon a stream;
Who hears the words they utter, who sees their transient gleam?
They pass by lonely rivers, they weep by cold dim seas,
Gates where the lost soul shivers are fanned by wings of these.
They are blossoms born of summer, yet beings of Earth's breath,
Not man, the latest comer—but old as Love or Death!
The first lips softly meeting, the first fierce swift heart-beat,
In these their life was beating, a bitter life and sweet.
They die, but are immortal; they go, but come again;
From portal unto portal they gather joy and pain.
Dim shores of dreams behold them, pale plumaged as a dove,
Out of the dusk enfold them white wings of Death or Love;

Though Heaven receive them never, though God make Night of Day,
Through years and years for ever they sought, and seek the way;
Souls upon souls kept under, pale spirits purple-crowned,
They smite the seas in sunder, they search the whole world round,
Yet find not Love unchanging, nor Life that drives out Death,
But bright wings briefly ranging, a red moth's hour of breath.
Sleep, goal of all things human, for flower and beast and bird,
For love of man and woman, for might of deed and word!
Sleep, Night, and Silence only, and sound of falling rain,
No waking to feel lonely, no dreams that day makes vain;
Though heart on heart reposes, or heart from heart lies far,
What care, once sunset closes the door morn sets ajar!
What matter what our choice is, since only Death's the right!
Nay, answer! flower-soft voices, out of the mists of night;
Is there, oh sister flowers, one gleam of dawn above?
Alas, but long dark hours, and falling tears of Love!

He cares not for your clinging, is soothed not by your song,
And fainter grows your singing—The Night, the Night is long!
With drenched wet tresses trailing, with purple garments torn,
You look, with eyes now failing, for dim grey streaks of morn;
But hours that have no number run through the glass of Night—
A heavier spell than slumber, a stronger sense than sight,
Comes down on these dim valleys and makes my waiting vain:
I seal my heart's fair chalice up, its rapture and its pain.

VIII

THE OFFERING

WHAT of all gifts shall I give
   Unto the heart of my love?
Stars from the ether above?
   Clouds that the storm-spirits weave?
Should I their loveliness prove
   Worthy for her to receive,
Is there a gift I can give
   Unto the heart of my love!

Down in the depths of the deep,
   Low in the caves of the sea,
There could my soul wander free,
   Treasures to gather and heap,
Pearls purely lovely as she,
   Precious as tears she might weep.
Should I their loveliness prove
   Worthy for her to receive,
Is there a gift I can give
   Unto the heart of my love!

Gems from deep earth brought to light,
    Gay with all glorious hues,
Not such as these would she choose—
    Ah, what would gladden her sight?
Hark, while my vexed soul pursues,
    Warbles the minstrel of night;
"Dost thou Love's loveliness prove
    Worthy for her to receive,
Love is the gift thou canst give
    Unto the heart of thy love!"

IX

THE ROSE

On my belovèd's heart at morn
   A rose lay, dew-empearled;
She said, and blushed the flower to scorn,
   "Thy love is worth the world:
      Ah, yes,
   Thy love is worth the world!"

Upon her weary heart at eve
   The dead rose-leaves were furled;
She said, "Yet did not hope deceive:
   Thy love was worth the world;
      Through all,
   Thy love was worth the world."

X

THE ROSE AND THE STAR

To a rose of the summer weather
   Sang a star of the summer night,
"Oh come, let us shine together
   In the gloom of this lonely height;
Oh rise with thy hues resplendent
   To him thou dost love so well,
For all lights in the heavens pendant
   Shall my sweet star-rose excel!"

But the rose in the valley's hollow
   Cried up through the night, "Oh, star!
I cannot arise and follow,
   For the way is weary and far;
Oh leap from thy place thus lonely
   In measureless space above,
And fly for one moment only
   To the heart of thine earthly love!"

So she cried in this mournful fashion
    Through the hush of the dark cool air,
And the star, grown pale with passion,
    Sprang down at her plaintive prayer ;
And he flashed, as a meteor flashes,
    To her arms with a great glad shout,
But the rose was turned to ashes,
    And the flame of the star burnt out.

XI

THE TEMPLE OF FAME

Oh, Wisdom! high throned in far silence, where stars are
    the steps of thy throne,
What crown wilt thou weave him a while hence, my lord,
    and my god, and my own?
What wreath of thy gardens preparing, in regions un-
    kissed of the sun?
What immortelles too cold for man's wearing, that heroes
    have worshipped and won?
Wilt thou write in the fires of the spheres his name when
    I breathe it no more,
And his eyes cease from gladness and tears, and his soul
    from the search of thy lore?
When the earth lies like lead on our hearts, when our
    earth, when our mother, again
Bids us heed not what season departs, what summers
    may waxen and wane;
When we grow as the clay of the fields, as the stones of
    the desolate hill,
And above us the flashing of shields, the power, and the
    might, and the will—

Brave deeds and true love, all the story of men as we share in it now!—
Then the world shall shout forth to his glory, the nations before him shall bow!
Oh, Wisdom! though lips that are living breathe passionate words in his ear,
While fresh is the praise of thy giving, they are silenced since many a year;
Though they speak, bending low at thine altar, of one who sought truth to the end,
Whose steps would not weary, nor falter, nor cease evermore to ascend,
Who lightened the darkness of things, revealing the workings of God,
And climbed to the source of His springs, the heights of His mountains untrod,
Shall the love of his life be forgot, the hours unbidden of fame,
When knowledge and science were not, and the strength of the heart overcame,
When under the stars of the south he spoke with a daughter of men,
And sweet were the words of his mouth, and fair were the ferns of the glen;—

. . . .

I have loved thee; go forth—be immortal; shall we sleep the less sound for their praise,

When outside the dark hush of our portal they crown
    the cold marble with bays!
Ah, better is Now than Hereafter, is Love than the
    wisdom of years,
And sweeter the season of laughter, of kisses paid freely
    for tears,
Than a name in men's mouths who shall follow and
    point where the faint footsteps are,
Till they vanish where echo the hollow dull thunders of
    ocean afar!—
O Wisdom, high throned in far silence, though stars be
    the steps of thy throne,
Fair crowns thou mayest weave him a while hence: to-day
    I have crowned him my own.

XII

A SONG OF A GARDEN

I PLANTED a rose; let the tender leaves close,
Soul-thrilled at a kiss, when the honey bees settle,
Be it red as the dawn is, or pale as the snows,
Till the deep perfumed cup of its heart overflows
To the music that out of the summer night grows;—
But the rose of my planting has turned to a nettle!

I planted a lily—how slowly and stilly
The soul of the flower should grow in the gloom,
When winds over Spring's tender greenness blow chilly,
In the noontide of stars, one star-flower should fill the
Dim garden with glory. Alas! for my lily!
The cold scarlet poppies grew up in its room!

The purple-crowned flower, Love's passionate dower,
I planted one day with a vow in my heart;
And I dreamed it should climb as a serpent in power,
Till its blossoms should crown me, its leaves be my bower,
A holy pavilion in sunshine and shower—
There rose but a thorn that pierced deep as a dart!

And I looked on the fruit, and my heart was the root
Of the harvest of anguish that mocked me at last;
When spring-time and sowing are far from pursuit,
When the fields have grown gold, and the nightingales
    mute,
Shall we plant in that day, till the green tendrils shoot?
Alas! but the day of our planting is past!

But the flowers of my dreams I shall find by the streams
Of the great sunless world whither swiftly I go;
I shall gather the pale-petalled harvest that seems
As twilight to noontide, as stars to sunbeams;
I shall know if an ocean of weeping redeems
One hour of living—too late I shall know!

XIII

A SONG OF LOVE AND DEATH

To my heart's door an angel came:
  "Dost thou not know me, child?" he said.
As sound of music was his name,
  A halo shone about his head;
  With stars his robe was fashionèd,
And wrought with lightning and with flame;
  His face was paler than the dead,
  My life was glad through words he said,
    The hour he came, the hour he came!

To my heart's door an angel came:
  "I wait to take thee hence," he said;
And, lo! his eyes were fierce like flame,
  A kingly crown was on his head,
  And in his hand a sword blood-red,
As sound of weeping was his name,
  And he was shrouded like the dead;
  My life waxed dim through words he said,
    The hour he came, the hour he came!

XIV

REMEMBRANCE

Who sings of summer-time,
  When Earth, grey-veiled in frost,
  Is like a soul that's lost,
  Or love some hand has tossed
Away before its prime?

If, in her shroud of ice,
  She sleeps, and dreams of when
  Flowers, like the lives of men,
  Grew up in field and glen,
With breath of spice—

If her pale dream recalls
  The rose's heart of flame,
  The sweet rose-soul that came,
  Answering her loveliest name,
Through June's dew-falls—

If she remember these,
    Shall we, whose June day's wove,
    With murmurs of the dove,
    And stars and roses, love,
—Recall no ecstasies!
    Oh, sleepy cypress grove,
    Dreaming beneath thy trees,
    We will remember these!.

XV

A MELODY

WHAT song for thee my dreams can weave?
  What words would teach thee to believe,
How, changeless under changing skies,
  My heart within thy keeping lies,
Striving to hold from morn to eve,
  The hour that still remorseless flies.

The hours that fly, the love that stands,
  And gathers flowers with eager hands,
Till shadows lengthen on the grass,
  And the hills grow a dusky mass,
And moaning o'er the summer lands,
  The eternal, last "Adieu" must pass.

But from thy side I will not stray,
  Through all the green and golden day,
Short may it be or long, and yet
  Shall find us, as when first we met,
The eventide that melts away
  In darkness where no suns are set.

XVI

A REQUIEM

Lost, lost, for ever lost!
   Dead, dead, for ever dead!
Weary and tempest-tossed,
   Here rest thine head;
Here on this rocky bed,
   Life, hope, and love are fled—
All, all for ever lost,
   All, all is dead!

Sweet, sweet, Love's lips to thee—
   Deep, deep, his eyes;
Deep as the shoreless sea,
   Deep as the skies—
He shall no more arise,
   Steeping thy soul in sighs;
Lost, lost, his lips to thee;
   Closed, closed, his eyes!

XVII

"SI JEUNESSE SAVAIT"

Oh that the song of Love were ever new!
Oh that his plumy wings were clipped from ranging,
That the sweet rose might bloom with morning dew,
Through all the noontide heat, the long hours' changing.
Oh that the eyes that love us might not see
The shadow of the years upon us falling;
How small a terror even Death would be,
If from some sheltering hold we heard him calling.

What if Love leave us as the long years wane,
And all the smiles that wooed him once are faded!
Ah, not one day of joy returns again:
Their grave is some dim dreamland, cypress-shaded.
Drink deep of summer while the roses stay,
And nightingales sing sweet among the roses,
So shall remembrance waft thy soul away,
When the long year in bleak December closes.

XVIII

TO A BABY

GLAD eyes of blue!
 What holds the world before you as its prize?
What promise, false or true,
 Shall sorrow darken you,
Or shall you shine with triumph, radiant eyes?

Oh little head!
 What crown shall deck your waves of sunny brown?
Green laurels, roses red,
 Or white flowers for the dead?
Or all these make, oh little head, your crown!

Sweet mouth and small!
 Have you received the gift of gracious speech?
That all things base may fall,
 All spirits hear your call;
Oh little mouth, what great truth shall you teach?

Oh little hands!
   What gifts has Fate to fill your tiny clutch?
What mission waiting stands,
   What work in many lands
For these to do? Ah me, so much, so much.

Oh twinkling feet!
   What paths of pilgrimage for you are set?
Where roses blossom sweet,
   Or thorns your steps defeat,
—Dear little feet, my hands enclose you yet!

Oh little heart,
   So fond, so glad, so innocent of guile!
Will all your grace depart
   In life's tumultuous mart?
Nay, for such gifts all life's too brief a while.
       Oh little heart!

XIX

AT A LIFE'S END

Out through the gate of birth
   Came the star-eyed soul of a child;
And life and the joy of Earth
   Was sweet to him, and he smiled.

Hope met him first on his way,
   And nursed him on her knee.
"How long and bright was the day,
   How wide the sparkling sea!"

His eyes gave back her smile;
   He nestled to her breast;
"Oh, the glad hours, the long, long while,
   And her heart his haven of rest!"

Toil tore him far from the breast of Hope;
   Love gave him tears for bread;
And the gates of the Temple of Fame set ope
   Gleamed mocking over his head.

He gave his heart for a stone,
    His name for a crown of brass,
And at even time he lay alone
    On a waste of seeding grass.

He thought of hope, long lost;
    Of joy, long danced away;
Of red rose blossoms of Eden, tossed
    In the dust of his heedless way.

And, as he thought, the tears
    Rose up in his arid eyes;
He had planted out in the years,
    And the fruit of his life was lies.

There came a form to his side;
    A hand stole into his own;
Out of the whole world wide
    There spoke one voice alone.

"Lie, weary head, on my breast,
    More soft than the white-plumed dove
Oh, heart, that hast found no rest,
    Find rest on the heart of Love!"

Night fell on them like a veil,
    And the shoreless starry sea
Rolled on till the dawn gleamed pale
    As a soul out of night set free.

But these from their place were gone,
    And whither no man knows :
One faded rose lay white and wan,
    On the place of that last repose.

XX

THROUGH HOPE TO SLEEP

Hope, in the birth and the forthcoming
    Out of the void,
Out of the sleep-spell cold and numbing,
Into the noise of life-wheels humming,
    Wheels of life in the waste up-buoyed;
Out of the dusk of a dreamland dreary,
The eyes undimmed and the feet unweary,
    In through the gates by the Fates set ope,
Gates of Birth on the shores of Sorrow,
Pain to welcome us, fear to borrow,
Yet is our name for the nameless morrow
              Hope!

Love in the day of Life's fulfilling
    Crowned with delight,
Hours when the wheels their clamour stilling
Wait for the voice of music thrilling
    Souls of stars in the starry night;

THROUGH HOPE TO SLEEP

Love, all giving and all forgiving,
Out of the weary ways of living,
Finding rest in the sacred grove.
Garden of God on the skirts of Earth,
The pain of Death and the travail of Birth,
Are worth thee! What hadst thou not been worth,
    Love!

Sleep, far from dreams, that rocks the tired
 Soul, at the last;
Sleep, not as Hope, with smiles attired,
Not crowned as Love, the long desired,
 For these sleep too with the worn-out Past,
The budding branch and the full fruition
Are shades too dim for our recognition,
Since eyes grown heavy cannot weep,
Tears grow too weary for our shedding,
Fate in the dusk a couch is spreading,
And tired Life for ever wedding
    Sleep.

XXI

AN ANTHEM OF MORTALITY

From the rose-leaf that is shed,
From the forest, leafless, dead,
From extinguished worlds o'erhead,
Hark, the cry is still the same—
Life create, the vital flame
All a fair creation filling,
Rising, with deep passion thrilling,
Rising, opening like a flower,
Life, joy, rapture—for an hour!
Ending in a slow decay,
All its glories pass away,
From their bright summit hurled to be
Thy victims, fell Mortality!
Ah, God, and shall we nothing save?
Each prayer a requiem, every heart a grave!

Worlds on worlds grown cold and colder!
Stars that mock the sad beholder!
Was there warmth and life in you,
Life that never shall renew,

In your cold rocks and silent seas?
Ah me, that all things end like these!
Oh, rose that blushest so, I take
Thee to my heart: there may it break,
Pressed to thy thorns.   Sweet, let us die
Ere darkens round us earth and sky!
Who knows if there is One who grieves
O'er my lost hopes, thy falling leaves.
Oh, rose of roses, joy of joys;
Oh, voice heard clear above the noise,
The deafening noise of Earth, thou chief
Of all things beautiful and brief;
Art thou too fainter?   Oh, sweet flower,
Offspring of summer's golden hour,
Fad'st thou?—Ah, let the winds that shake
Thy petals from their shelter, take
My life with these, and let them lie
Scattered upon me as I die.
Sweet rose, more sweet in every thorn,
O'er thee and me the woods shall mourn,
The wet winds sigh, the wan stars weep,
The stream lament beside us: Sleep
Upon my heart, sweet rose, nor sever
Thyself from me till both must end for ever.

XXII

SONNET

PYGMALION'S DREAM

Zeus! I thank thee for the gift of her,
My fairest thought, the better part of me,
Whose face is rosier than the dawn-red sea,
And in whose eyes life's new-born raptures stir;
She counts not years by human calendar;
But Love, who made and chained her, set her free
From the cold marble's voiceless mastery:
So came the maiden soul—sweet wanderer!

And where the white stone glistened in the sun
Carved round her brow, her sun of golden hair
Makes morning lovely; and the sightless stare
Becomes blue depths where magic currents run;
But best of all, my love, my only one,
To clasp thee to my heart and hold thee there!

XXIII

SONNET

THE FULFILMENT

Zeus! take back the soul, the life, the blood,
And give me back my changeless masterpiece;
For when Time's flight bids Love's enchantments cease,
What hath life left of beautiful or good?
When she, my perfect dream, before me stood,
And blessed me for life's gift and Love's release,
I saw not then the statue's deathless peace
Lost in the fading bloom of womanhood.

The smooth unwrinkled marble of her breast
Had looked as lovely to my gaze to-day;
No furrows from her brow to smooth away,
No worn-out eyes to make love seem a jest.
Alas! 'twas mine own ruin I caressed,
And my fame fades with tresses that grow grey!

XXIV

SONNET

Rose, of the dewy cluster that he sent,
The loveliest and the last, whose crushed perfume
Of crimson petals, in my twilight room,
Kindles a sweetness unto sorrow blent;
For when the dew was fresh on thee I bent
Mine eyes with dew of tears above thy bloom,
Last messenger across the desolate gloom,
What time my life was darkened, and he went.

But, oh! my rose, close pressed twixt page and page
Of this heart-treasured book—oh! shall it be
That some day, looking on its leaves with me,
He who first sent shall see thee, sorrow's gage,
And smile for new strange joy, whose pilgrimage
Shall pass where roses bloom unceasingly.

XXV

SONNET

When lays the soul the body's garment by,
And ventures forth to meet the great Perhaps,
Whether he rest his head on houris' laps,
Or through pale grasses watch a dream-pale sky,
Or kneel before the Seraph's ceaseless cry
Beside the Tree of Life no canker saps,
Where Godhead's triune mystery enwraps
The heart of all things made, the mighty Why.

What matter, lives unlived and worlds untrod,
After this Earth, where we would yet remain,
Wringing a little pleasure out of pain;
This is the end, beneath the grass-grown sod;
And for each spirit in the Courts of God,
A dead, cold heart lies silent in the rain.

XXVI

LIFE

His journey begins through the world—ah me,
What a long, long way to go!
Over mountain and desert away to the sea,
Through springtide blooms to the snow.

And youth with its gladness, and beauty's crown
Come forth as the years go by,
And the blossoms pale of the flower Renown
Unfold 'neath the summer sky.

But the landscape changes, the light grows dim
The sea is a deep dark grave—
Oh, let one star be a sign to him
Of a day-dawn over the wave!

XXVII

FAILURE

I CANNOT set my weary feet
   Upon the slopes that looked so near,
But ever more and more retreat
   While the leaves glide from green to sere,
     Through Time's swift beat.

The day shall never come to me
   Upon the mountain top to stand,
And watch the blue, incurving sea
   Embrace the wild, pine-wooded land :
     —It cannot be.

Once dreamed I that unto my view
   All lovely lands should lie outspread ;
Who reach the top are very few,
   And ashes of the nameless dead
     The track bestrew.

Oh, pilgrim, if that summit high
    You reach, forget not that I strove;
When life, its end attained, must die,
    Forget not then the dream I wove
        Of that pure sky.

Though your eyes see what mine forego,
    The wondrous world beneath your feet,
From your cold throne of dawn-red snow,
    Where ways of man with God's ways meet,
        That no men know,

Yet think, far down the mountain slope,
    My feet have slipped, my heart grown cold;
I shared your path in youth and hope;
    Alone you watch God's worlds unrolled,
        Their gates set ope.

XXVIII

IN THE GARDEN OF THE SHADOW

SHALL this be the end of their glory and passion?
Oh, Sea, with thy million of voices declare
If these children of earth are but formed in the fashion
Of flowers, for one day made radiant and fair.
Did they live in the ages long past, or hereafter
Shall they come to exist as the world circles on,
And youth has its season of playtime and laughter,
And age fades away in the mists, and is gone?
Shall they dwell among men with no dream of past
    meeting,
Their souls in new forms that the ages bring forth?
From a long sleep of darkness tumultuously greeting
Our world, new and fair from the South to the North?
Shall they stretch forth glad hands to each other,
    exclaiming,
"Oh, welcome to Love, long unknown and now met!"
And dream all things else but base metal, and framing
This jewel of love in their worthlessness set?

And then shall they crown their fair heads with the roses,
A million times bloomed, and a million times dead,
Since to-day, when so swiftly their pilgrimage closes
And on their white faces the sunrise glows red!
Or in sleep that is dreamless and pulseless for ever,
Shall they lie under earth till with earth they are one,
And Science and Art and all mighty endeavour
Call loudly above them as centuries run?
But dust among dust they are scattered and shaken,
As rose petals trampled by hurrying feet—
Who pities the rose-leaves all brown and forsaken,
Or sees through their ashes that once they were sweet?
The passionless mountains are strong and abiding,
But fierce-beating hearts have one hour—no more!
As they leave the dim threshold of birth, they are gliding
Where Death's muffled form guards the terrible door;
And Love, the chief good, the chief joy of our living,
Stretches hands out to stay them who may not be stayed.
Ah! surely the gods need from us most forgiving,
Who bring to such anguish the creatures they made!
Ah, surely they heed not! and Death, the Immortal,
Leads Love a frail captive and binds him with chains,
Till his face waxes white in the shade of the portal,
And his servants go hence, and he only remains.

XXIX

RONDEL

Long ago, as one awake from sleeping
Sees a dream recalled pale memories dimly show,
Strange thy love and dim, and looks through shadows
    creeping—
        Long ago.

All is grey with clouds—I cannot see nor know;
Yet may sheltering wings o'erspread us in safe keeping!
On the cloud's dark rim there burns a golden glow.

They that sow in tears shall come to joyous reaping.
When glad voices, mingling, murmur low,
" Far away it seems, that weary time of weeping—
        Long ago!"

XXX

RONDEL

YESTERDAY! ah me, what vain recalling,
When the first rose opened out in May,
And the nightingales brought songs enthralling—
    Yesterday!

Summer flowers adorn no wintry way;
Snows upon their barren grave are falling;
Brief as love and gladness was their stay;

And the voice of exiled Love is calling,
Over frozen deserts cold and grey,
"Death had been the kindest fate befalling—
    Yesterday."

XXXI

RONDEL

But To-morrow comes, for which attending
Still I wait; oh! Time needs not to borrow;
Soon To-day and Yesterday are blending—
    But To-morrow!

Weeping, we have sown the weary furrow;
Shall the harvest moon, through Summer's night ascending,
Shine on garnered sheaves, the waiting weeks gone through?

Sheaves with golden fruit to earth that bore them bending,
Songs of harvest joy from throats that ached with sorrow—
Not To-day, on heart or hope depending—
    But To-morrow!

XXXII

RONDEL

STILL, Good night, although no voice replying
Comes through blackness of the starless height,
Over leagues of dark seas rocked in sighing—
        Still, Good night !

Sleep, beloved, in peace till morning light,
Hear in dreams my heart that unto thine is crying ;
See mine eyes that weep for exile from thy sight ;

May God keep thee till the lone days flying
   Pass, and, by an ocean infinite,
Meet we in the land of Love undying—
        Still, Good night !

XXXIII

SERENADE

Oh my heart, oh my heart!
Let us live before we part
In a garden of Love's planting,
In a kingdom of his granting,
—Where the unfathomed purple night
Draws up rapture out of sight
Till it clasps the infinite
Soul of Love from whence thou art,
    Oh my heart, oh my heart!

Oh my love, oh my love!
Shadows on the terrace move,
Shadows of the world foregone,
Of the faith we lean not on,
Of long years lived through in vain,—
But they pass, and we remain
Dreaming that the stars shall wane
Ere one colder kiss we prove,
    Oh my love, oh my love!

Oh my heart, oh my heart!
Pluck the rose and dare the smart
Of the thorns around it set—
Disillusion and regret!
—Men have found them bitter,—No!
As two streams unite, and flow,
One broad river sea-wards—so
From this hour our lives shall start,
    Oh my heart, oh my heart.

Oh my love, oh my love!
Thou hast glories dreamed not of
Set in eyes that I look through
As the sun looks on the dew
In the rose's cup of fire,
—Oh my heart's, my soul's desire,
In thy gold hair's rich attire!
Life, and all the joy thereof,
    Oh my love, oh my love!

Oh my heart, oh my heart!
—Stars may fail, and downward dart
Burning out to utter death,
So may passion's fiery breath
Leave our warm hearts cold and blind,
Leave our arms no more entwined,
Bid the long spell cease to bind
—Not together—nor apart,
    Oh my heart, oh my heart!

SERENADE

Oh my love, oh my love!
Thou whose lightest whisper drove
All things from my heart but thee,
Lost me in a soundless sea!
—If this hour of joy must pass
To the silence under grass—
Drain the wine and break the glass!
Sleep, while yet the charm be wove,
    Oh my love, oh my love.

XXXIV

HYMN

Oh Thou most far from joy or sorrow,
    From hope or fear!
Lord of the Night-time and the Morrow,
    Far things and near.
Oh Thou unseen of us, nor ever
    Known good or ill,
Though thy hand plant and thy sword sever
    Life's fruit at will,—
We know Thee not for God or Devil,
    For friend or foe,
We only know the seed is evil,
    The fruit is woe.

We gave Thee worship in green places
    From sea to sea,
And downward looked with patient faces
    For sign of Thee,

We said, "Thou art the wide sea's thunder,
    The still shore's rest,
And the cold sleep that draws us under
    Is but Thy breast!"—
Our life-blood flowed, the white world staining
    Beneath Thy feet,
Still on, through waxing years and waning,
    Through cold and heat,
We sought Thee, God to help us, Mortal
    To share our throes,
But now, before Thy thrice-barred portal,
    Who knows! who knows!

The cold, deep Earth, where sleep unwaking
    Awaits all heads,
Is more than Thou, for unforsaking
    Her arm outspreads.
She gathers to her breast the falling,
    The withered leaves;
The lives whose bloom is past recalling,
    She knows and grieves.
She takes the songless birds, the tired
    Strained hearts that break,
The loves unwept and undesired,
    The years' long ache,—
All grief she gathers and assuages
    In dreamless sleep;

Her night is made of circling ages,
    Her bed is deep.
They hear no bitter sentence spoken
    Her babes at rest,
The wounded spirits Thou hast broken
    Faint on her breast.
Oh Earth! oh fruitful, holy Mother,
    Star-eyed and still!
In Heaven nor Hell there is no other
    To save or kill.
Hell is too deep, too high Heaven's portal,
    Too far God's throne,
And kisses of Love's lips immortal
    As dreams are flown.
All dies, all fades, all swiftly passes,
    Even Faith's firm hand,
Brief as the life of meadow-grasses
    Our days are spanned.
Alas for Love that may not linger!
    For dreams undone!
For broken lute and silent singer
    Beneath the sun.
Alas for blind faith meekly kneeling
    In restful prayer!
—For our disease is Life—our healing,
    Oh Earth!—lies there.

XXXV

SUNSET-LAND

Into Sunset-land
 Through a red-gold mist,
 You and I will float,
 Learning, hand in hand,
 All the tune we missed,
 Perfect, note to note,
  In the Sunset-land.

In a living fire,
 In a golden sea,
 You and I will glide,
 Seeing, side by side,
 Our attained desire
 As a god set free
 Passing on flame-fanned
  Into Sunset-land.

All the weary shore,
 All the bitter tide,
 Lose themselves at last
 Where the light runs fast

Wider and more wide,
Burning evermore,
Loosening band on band,
    Spreads the Sunset-land.

Cold as lonely rocks
    Frozen hearts draw nigh
    To that shore's embrace,
    Love the gate unlocks
    Where rose-gardens lie,
    Sun-roses round the space
    Where his shrine doth stand
        In the Sunset-land.

In the rapturous light
    Roses gold and red,
    Roses red and gold,
    Sweet as dreams of old,
    Crown Love's drooping head,
    Heal his failing sight,—
    —We shall understand
        In the Sunset-land.

XXXVI

SONNET

GOOD-NIGHT

Farewell, good-night! the terraced garden lies
All white beneath the moon, in sighing sleep,
—The sea looms as a shadow, but the skies
Draw near us, heart to heart, and deep to deep,
Till weeping Love clings close to stars that weep,
And all the purple Night, dissolved in sighs,
Lays her immortal hand on weary eyes,—
—Oh Night beloved! one memory for us keep!

Oh rapturous Austral night of stars and scent!
My life is but a passing dream of thine
Who countest not the fires of stars outspent
As ages circle round thy deathless shrine,
—Yet dear as dearest love and nearest sight,
Thy voice speaks low to me: " Farewell, good-night."

Sydney, 1894.

XXXVII

ENVOI

Oh, Love, for evermore in blessing blest,
Star of all stars! shine on us through the years!
In weary wandering ways be thou our rest;
When gloom enshrouds us, o'er the mountain crest
Arise, and lead us through the vale of tears.

www.ingramcontent.com/pod-product-compliance
Lightning Source LLC
Chambersburg PA
CBHW031604110426
42742CB00037B/1066